'Kya Aap Paanchvi Pass Se Tez Hain?', is the exciting new studio based game show hosted by the inimitable Shah Rukh Khan.

The game is all about competing for the huge sum of Rs. 5 crore, by answering correctly questions taken from primary school syllabus- Grade 1 to Grade 5.

Each individual contestant is presented with 10 subject cards which can be answered in any order. Each correct answer takes you higher up on the Rupee ladder. Answering 5 questions correctly gets you Rs. 2,00,000 but if you give a wrong answer before that, you leave with nothing.

Now this quiz book, inspired by 'Kya Aap Paanchvi Pass Se Tez Hain?', offers you the chance to play this exciting game right at home.

Each correct answer gets you a bagful of money! So gather all your friends, play the Paanchvi Pass game and see who wins the Rs. 5 crore prize!!

Happy Gaming!

Quiz 1

Q1 What were Mumbai, Kolkata and Chennai earlier known as?

Q2 What is the most essential component of the air you breathe in?

Q3 The easiest way to tell the difference between an African and an Asian elephant is by the size of its...

A) Tusks
B) Feet
C) Eyes
D) Ears

Q4 If you give the shopkeeper Rs. 20 note for an eraser worth Rs. 3.25 and a pencil worth Rs. 2.50, how much money should be returned?

A) Rs. 13.25
B) Rs. 15.25
C) Rs. 14.25
D) Rs. 14.50

Q5 What is not a part of the nervous system?

A) Nerves
B) Brain
C) Heart

PLAY-AT-HOME
QUIZ BOOK

Airtel
Presents

Kya aap
PAANCHVI PASS
se tez hain?

Published 2008 by
Prakash Books India Pvt. Ltd.
1, Ansari Road, Daryaganj
New Delhi 110 002, India.
E-mail: sales@prakashbooks.com
Website: www.prakashbooks.com
Tel: 91-11-23247062-65

ISBN: 978-81-7234-283-8

PLAY-AT-HOME
QUIZ BOOK

Airtel
Presents

Kya aap
PAANCHVI PASS
se tez hain?

Q6 What is the path of a planet's revolution around the Sun called?

5 lakh

Q7 What is the adverb in the following sentence?

"The waitress moved briskly through the crowded restaurant."

10 lakh

Q8 What is the major component of bones and teeth?

20 lakh

Q9 What is located at Cape Kennedy in the USA?

50 lakh

Q10 Kidneys and the lungs help the body to eliminate wastes. Which other part does the same?

1 Crore

Q11 According to the World Health Organization, which disease is considered eradicated?

A) Chicken Pox
B) Tuberculosis
C) Smallpox
D) Influenza

5 Crore

Quiz 2

Q1 If large, larger and largest is in order, then what's missing in loud, _____ and loudest? 10,000/-

Q2 What is the official language of India? 20,000/-

Q3 What is the decimal form of 274 / 1000? 50,000/-

Q4 If you bought 6 boxes containing 24 apples each, how many bags containing 6 apples each could I make using these apples? 1 lakh

A) 20
B) 24
C) 22
D) 23

Q5 What is locomotion? 2 lakh

Q6 What is the other name for Harmandir Sahib, a Sikh Shrine?

5 lakh

Q7 What is soil made of?

10 lakh

Q8 What is the main function of flowers?

20 lakh

Q9 What is another name for a plateau?

50 lakh

Q10 Indus Valley Civilization was spread over...

A) Punjab & Sind
B) Along Indus River
C) Punjab & Jammu
D) Sind & Rajasthan

1 Crore

Q11 Arthashastra was written by Chanakya.

True or False?

5 Crore

Quiz 3

Q1 What is the plural of saucer? 10,000/-

Q2 What is the plural of ox? 20,000/-

Q3 What is the closest star to earth? 50,000/-

Q4 If you are "all thumbs", basically you are? 1 lakh

A) Stupid
B) Clumsy
C) Funny
D) Careful with your hands

Q5 What is another word for a hurricane? 2 lakh

A) Tornado
B) Twister
C) Water spout
D) Cyclone

Q6 What is the opposite of frequently?

5 lakh

Q7 What is measured in cubic metres?

10 lakh

Q8 What is the interest earned on Rs. 12000 at 5% p.a. for 3 years?

20 lakh

Q9 What is a group of peacocks called?

50 lakh

Q10 In which year was the first railway line in India opened?

A) 1853
B) 1861
C) 1836
D) 1835

1 Crore

Q11 Bathometer is used to measure the proportinate area to be allocated to bathrooms in any house.

True or False?

5 Crore

Quiz 4

Q1 Which of the following animals is aerial?

10,000/-

A) Fish
B) Camel
C) Bird
D) Monkey

Q2 What is the smallest two digit number?

20,000/-

Q3 What is the capital of Indonesia?

50,000/-

Q4 If the total of two numbers is 9875 and one of the number is 4899, then what is the other number?

1 lakh

Q5 What is a mythical creature with a lion's body and a woman's head in Egypt called?

2 lakh

A) Easter Island Statue
B) Sphinx
C) Phoenix
D) Narasimha

Q6 What is the one word to describe a person who knows many languages?

5 lakh

Q7 What is believed to be the source of the Ganga river? — 10 lakh

A) Gangotri
B) Gomukh
C) Mt. Kailash
D) Mansarovar

Q8 What is the female fox called? — 20 lakh

Q9 What is 1 hectare approximately equal to? — 50 lakh

A) 1 acre
B) 1.5 acres
C) 10 acres
D) 2.5 acres

Q10 In which quadrilaterals do the diagonals bisect and are equal? — 1 Crore

Q11 Before October 2003 which Indian state was marked as an independent country on the official website of China?

A) Arunachal Pradesh
B) Mizoram
C) Tripura
D) Sikkim

5 Crore

Quiz 5

Q1) There are 1275 trees in a garden of which 850 are of mango, 75 of coconut and remaining of jackfruit. What is the number of jackfruit trees?

10,000/-

A) 350
B) 925
C) 450
D) 250

Q2) What is the Taj Mahal made of?

20,000/-

Q3) What is the answer to a multiplication problem called?

50,000/-

Q4) If the cost of 8 notebooks is Rs. 72, what is the cost of 5 notebooks?

1 lakh

A) 36
B) 54
C) 45
D) 40

Q5) What expresses actions,events and/or states of beings about a noun?

2 lakh

Q6) What is the one word to describe a person who is too proud of himself?

5 lakh

Q7 What does the Parliament in India consist of? — 10 lakh

A) President & Lok Sabha
B) President & Rajya Sabha
C) President & Two Houses
D) Lok Sabha & Rajya Sabha

Q8 What is the extra food stored by plants called? — 20 lakh

Q9 What does the word bonafide mean in English? — 50 lakh

Q10 In what kind of forest, leaves of some trees fall at the beginning of summer? — 1 Crore

A) Deciduous
B) Evergreen
C) Thorny Scrub

Q11 A man walks 3 km in 1 hour. Find the distance he can travel in 18 minutes?

Quiz 6

Q1 Through two given points how many lines can we draw?

Q2 What is the young one of a deer called?

Q3 What is the adjective in this sentence?

"I love the blue sky."

Q4 If Supreme Court is the highest court in India, what is the highest court in each state known as?

Q5 What does WWF stand for?

Q6 What is the meaning of 'Don't cross the bridge before you come to it'?

Q7 What does the abbreviation eg. stand for?

Q8 What is the capital of Bulgaria?

Q9 What does S in UNESCO stand for?

Q10 In isosceles triangle, how many sides are equal?

A) Four
B) Two
C) Three
D) One

Q11 Charles Darnay, Sydney Carton & Doctor Manette are the characters from which classic novel?

A) David Copperfield
B) A Tale of Two Cities
C) Great Expectations
D) Oliver Twist

Quiz 7

Q1 What is 1 and 1/2 expressed as a decimal? 10,000/-

Q2 What is the young one of eagle called? 20,000/-

Q3 What is nine times thirteen? 50,000/-

Q4 If cooking apples weigh 100g each, how many would you get in a kilogram? 1 lakh

Q5 What does the tailor bird use to stitch the leaves to make its nest? 2 lakh

A) Needle
B) Thorns
C) Stems
D) Beak

Q6 What is the line that divides the object or figure into two identical halves called?

Q7 What does DC stand for in Washington DC?

Q8 What is starch?

Q9 What do you call a group of penguins?

Q10 How many singular nouns are there in the following sentence ?

"Billy went to the ballpark to see the Rangers play the Angels."

Q11 About how many different muscles are there in the human body?

A) 50
B) 500
C) 5,000
D) 50,000

Quiz 8

Q1 What is one -third expressed as a decimal? — 10,000/-

Q2 What is the young one of an owl called? — 20,000/-

Q3 What is found on grass in the morning after a clear winter night? — 50,000/-

Q4 If Americans call it French Fries, what do Britishers refer to it as? — 1 lakh

Q5 What do you mean by 'chewing the cud'?

Q6 What is the english name of 'Kanyakumari'?

Q7 What do animals and humans give plants?

Q8 What is plural form of radius?

Q9 What do Japanese call their country?

Q10 How many prime numbers are there between 10 and 30?

Q11 An exterior angle of a triangle is equal to the sum of two _________ angles.

Quiz 9

Q1 What is one-sixth of 72? 10,000/-

Q2 What part of the plant do fruits grow from? 20,000/-

A) Flowers
B) Stem
C) Root
D) Shoot

Q3 What is Burma officially called now? 50,000/-

Q4 If a radius of a circle increases 3 times then the diameter also increases or remains same? 1 lakh

Q5 What do you call the uniform time fixed for each country? 2 lakh

Q6) What is the electric, electronic and mechanical equipment that makes up a computer called?

5 lakh

Q7) What are the rivers that flow through Tamil Nadu?

10 lakh

A) Vaigai & Kaveri
B) Vaigai & Krishna
C) Kaveri & Krishna

Q8) What is chin music in cricket ?

20 lakh

A) Wide ball
B) Googly
C) LBW
D) Short delivery

Q9) What do all birds of prey have?

50 lakh

Q10) How many plants will be there in a circular bed whose outer edge measures 30 cm allowing 4 cm^2 for each plant?

1 Crore

Q11) Anti meridian and post meridian are __________words.

A) Greek
B) Indian
C) Roman
D) French

5 Crore

Quiz 10

Q1 What is the difference between 111 and 64?

Q2 What takes place to choose leaders to rule the country?

Q3 What is an eighth of 16?

Q4 How many zeroes are in the numeral for one million?

Q5 What do you call the plants that eat insects?

Q6 What is the closest meaning to the following...To worship the rising sun?

A) To salute the rising sun
B) To honour promising young people
C) To welcome coming events
D) To honour a man who attends office

Q7 Which river is not part of the eastern coastal plain?

A) Mahanadi
B) Godavari
C) Krishna
D) Narmada

10 lakh

Q8 What is a reflex angle?

20 lakh

Q9 What are fossils?

50 lakh

Q10 How many adjectives are there in this sentence?

"The brown fox ran hurriedly from the barking dogs, as the red sun rose in the East."

1 Crore

Q11 As __________ as a statue.

Complete this Figure of Speech.

5 Crore

Quiz 11

Q1 What is the instrument used to draw a circle? 10,000/-

Q2 What type of dancers dance on their toes? 20,000/-

Q3 What is added to the cake to make it rise? 50,000/-

Q4 How many verbs are there in the following sentence ? 1 lakh

"I am the leader, so do your work."

Q5 What do we get when we mix red and blue colour? 2 lakh

Q6 What is the capital of Arunachal Pradesh? 5 lakh

Q7 Volume of water increases when sugar is dissolved in it.

True or False?

Q8 What is a common end point of an angle called?

Q9 Two cars set out at the same time to a town 80 kms away. 1 car travels at 80 kms/hr, the other car at 40 kms/hr. How much longer does the slower car take?

Q10 Chhetri and Gurung are the major ethnic groups of which neighbouring country of India?

A) Bangladesh
B) Bhutan
C) Nepal
D) Sri Lanka

Q11 American English refers to it as a notebook. What do Britishers refer to it as?

Quiz 12

Q1 What is the lowest prime number?

Q2 What was Subhash Chandra Bose popularly known as?

Q3 What is a set of points extending infinitely in both directions called?

A) Line
B) Place
C) Line segment
D) Point

Q4 How many times can we subtract 7 from 143?

Q5 What award is given to a person who has just missed winning?

Q6 What is the advantage of the sloping shape of conifers? — 5 lakh

Q7 Uranium is used to produce thermal power. — 10 lakh

True or False?

Q8 What does BNHS stand for? — 20 lakh

Q9 To which group of plants does the mushroom belong to? — 50 lakh

Q10 As regular as a...

Complete this Figure of Speech — 1 Crore

Q11 At an examination 35% marks are required to pass. If the total marks are 500, how many marks should one secure just to pass?

A) 175
B) 250
C) 200
D) 300

5 Crore

Quiz 13

Q1 What is the other name for rectangle with four equal sides? 10,000/-

Q2 What were the last words of Mahatma Gandhi before he died? 20,000/-

Q3 What is a plain situated at a considerable height called? 50,000/-

Q4 How many seconds are there in an hour? 1 lakh

Q5 What are the words of a song also called? 2 lakh

Q6 What is meant by parasitic plant?

5 lakh

Q7 To which species does the Komodo dragon belong?

A) Amphibians
B) Reptiles
C) Birds
D) Insects

10 lakh

Q8 What do you call a group of Turkeys?

20 lakh

Q9 Three common multiples of 18 and 6.

A) 18,6,9
B) 18, 36, 6
C) 36, 54, 72
D) none

50 lakh

Q10 Anil Kumble, Javagal Srinath and one more Indian feature in the list of maximum number of ducks. Who is the third cricketer?

1 Crore

Q11 Convert the speed of 25 m/sec to km/hr.

5 Crore

Quiz 14

Q1 What kind of triangle has a 90-degree angle? 10,000/-

Q2 What would you call a large town? 20,000/-

Q3 What is a person who writes a software program called? 50,000/-

Q4 How many nouns are there in the following sentence ? 1 lakh

"The horse ran into the barn and ate a lot of oats."

Q5 What are the primary colors of the spectrum? 2 lakh

Q6 What is a skin specialist known as?

Q7 To which religion do the two sects 'Mahayana' and 'Hinayana' belong?

Q8 What do you call a baby spider?

Q9 The teacher explained the assignment carefully.

Identify the Adverb?

Q10 An overhead water tank when 2/5th filled contains 300 litres of water. How many litres of water will be there in the tank when 2/3rd filled?

Q11 Edible oil is extracted from walnuts.

True or False?

Quiz 15

Q1 Which is the smallest natural number? **10,000/-**

Q2 Where did the lamb follow Mary in the nursery rhyme? **20,000/-**

Q3 What is a person who sells flowers called? **50,000/-**

A) Grocer
B) Florist
C) Fruiterer
D) Horticulturist

Q4 How do the following terms describe animals? **1 lakh**

A) Terrestial
B) Aquatic
C) Amphibians
D) Arboreal

Q5 What are the Latitudes of the North and South Pole? **2 lakh**

Q6 What is a group of whales called? **5 lakh**

Q7 Thiruvananthapuram is a City built on how many hills? **10 lakh**

A) 7
B) 8
C) 9

Q8 Vinoba Bhave was the first Indian to win the Ramon Magsaysay Award for Community Leadership.

True or False?

20 lakh

Q9 The supplementary angle of an acute angle will always be __________.

50 lakh

Q10 After which Roman God is January, the first month of the year, named?

A) Juno
B) Jupiter
C) Juventas
D) Janus

1 Crore

Q11 Where is the famous Shore Temple located ?

A) Puri
B) Vishakhapatnam
C) Mamallapuram
D) Chennai

Quiz 16

Q1 You can put 23 chairs in six even rows of four.

Yes / No

Q2 Where do desert plants like cactus store water?

A) Leaves
B) Stems
C) Flowers
D) Fruits

Q3 What is a line segment drawn from the centre of the circle to any point on the circle called?

Q4 How do penguins keep warm?

Q5 What are angles measured in?

Q6 What is a giant grass with a hollow, wooden stem called?

5 lakh

Q7 The Triveni Sangam is the union of Ganga, Yamuna and which other river?

A) Ravi
B) Brahmaputra
C) Saraswati
D) Sutlej

10 lakh

Q8 Underwater plants have stomata.

True or False?

20 lakh

Q9 The river that does not flow through Andhra Pradesh _____.

A) Godavari
B) Krishna
C) Narmada

50 lakh

Q10 A square has an area of 441 square cm. Find the perimeter of the square?

1 Crore

Q11 Which gas is used in an electric bulb?

A) Oxygen
B) Helium
C) Hydrogen
D) Argon & Nirtogen

5 Cr

Quiz 17

Q1 You have saved up to buy a mountain bike which cost Rs 2000 when you first saw it. But the price has increased by 10% how much does it cost now?

10,000/-

Q2 Where would you put a comma in the following sentence?

Ria bought pears apples bananas and a big grapefruit.

20,000/-

Q3 What happens at the count of three, four in the rhyme One Two Buckle My Shoe?

50,000/-

Q4 How do animals get their minerals from the soil?

A) By walking
B) By breathing
C) By eating plants
D) by eating soil

1 lakh

Q5 What are Aesop's Fables known for?

2 lakh

Q6 What helps leaves trap the sun's energy?

5 lakh

A) Stomata
B) Mid-rib
C) Chlorophyll
D) Veins

Q7 The Rath Yatra takes place in which city?

10 lakh

Q8 Under which tree did Gautam Buddha attain Nirvana?

20 lakh

Q9 The Rig Veda contains details of what to be performed by people?

50 lakh

A) Yagna
B) Hymns
C) Rituals
D) Yoga

Q10 A ________________ of stars.
Add the collective noun.

1 Crore

Q11 A ________________ of goods.
Add the collective noun.

5 Crore

Quiz 18

Q1 How many right angles are there in a right angle triangle?

Q2 Where would you find a collection of books and newspapers?

Q3 What does fauna refer to ?

A) Mountains
B) Forests
C) Animals
D) Rivers

Q4 How do amphibians breathe in water?

A) Through their skin
B) Lungs
C) Through mouth
D) Through nose

Q5 What is glass made of? 2 lakh

Q6 What are the two things plants give humans and animals? 5 lakh

Q7 The Puri district in Orissa encompasses of which lake? 10 lakh

Q8 Tides are caused by the gravitational pull of the earth 20 lakh

True or False?

Q9 The remains of which Christian missionary are housed in a heritage monument in Goa? 50 lakh

A) St. Francis Xavier
B) Mother Teresa
C) Graham stewart Staines
D) St. Thomas

Q10 What is one -fifith of hundred? 1 Crore

Q11 A jar has a capacity for 8 litres of milk. How many 200 ml measures will be needed to fill it?

A) 40
B) 20
C) 4
D) 16

5 Crore

Quiz 19

Q1 How many tens in 210?

10,000/-

Q2 Where would you go with your family if you have to watch a movie?

20,000/-

Q3 What does a stick insect resemble?

A) A worm
B) A twig
C) A Caterpillar
D) A Leaf

50,000/-

Q4 He is a careless driver.

Identify the Adjective?

1 lakh

Q5 The underground home of whom is referred to as the air conditioned city?

A) Termites
B) Rats
C) Rabbits
D) Lizards

2 lakh

Q6 What are the lower Himalayas called?

A) Shivalik
B) Sahyadari
C) Western Ghats

5 lakh

Q7 The Portuguese come to Goa in?

10 lakh

A) 1510
B) 1410
C) 1610

Q8 The weight of 46 percent of the earth's crust is made up of which element?

20 lakh

A) Nitrogen
B) Carbon Dioxide
C) Oxygen
D) Helium

Q9 The first ozone hole in the middle layer of the earth's atmosphere was detected in which continent?

50 lakh

Q10 Which of the following is an insect?

1 Crore

A) Miillipede
B) Cockroach
C) Snail
D) Spider

Q11 Abhanga and Tribhanga are postures of which dance form?

A) Odissi
B) Kathak
C) Kuchipudi
D) Bharatnatyam

5 Crore

Quiz 20

Q1 How much is 14 times 5? 10,000/-

A) 65
B) 50
C) 75
D) 70

Q2 Which are the two months that have thirty one days consecutively? 20,000/-

Q3 What do you get, when you mix yellow and blue? 50,000/-

Q4 Give an example of parallel lines in transportation? 1 lakh

Q5 The second longest river emerging from the Himalayas is... 2 lakh

A) Ganga
B) Yamuna
C) Brahmaputra
D) Indus

Q6 What are animals that eat other animals called? 5 lakh

Q7 The least number of 4 digits which are exactly divisible by 13 is. 10 lakh

Q8 The remains of the Vijayanagar empire can be found in...

20 lakh

A) Bijapur
B) Golconda
C) Hampi
D) Baroda

Q9 The birthday of which sportsperson is celebrated as National Sports Day ?

50 lakh

A) Prakash Padukone
B) Dhyan Chand
C) Sunil Gavaskar
D) P.T. Usha

Q10 What part of the plant caries water and salts to the rest of the plant?

1 Crore

Q11 What is batik?

A) A method of dyeing
B) A miniature painting
C) A form of sculpture
D) A type of weave in textiles

5 Crore

Quiz 21

Q1 If 23 - x = 2. Then x = ?

Q2 Which bird can rotate its head by 180 degree on either side?

Q3 What do you call a group of hummingbirds?

Q4 Form one word using the letters of "red & sip".

Q5 The planet Mercury stands between Venus and Mars.
True or False?

6) Uttarayan is the festival of what in Gujarat?

7) The first ever Railway line in India was opened between Bombay and Pune.

True or False?

8) The red blood cells carry ________ and ________.

9) The basic Roman numeral that can never be subtracted is.

10) In the word "stone," which letter is silent?

11) Which city is the capital of the new state of Jharkhand ?

A) Hazaribagh
B) Dhanbad
C) Jamshedpur
D) Ranchi

Quiz 22

Q1 If 6 + n = 15, What is n?

10,000/-

Q2 Which city is called the 'financial capital' of India?

20,000/-

Q3 What do the doctors use to listen to the sounds in the chest and adbomen?

50,000/-

Q4 Find a similar meaning word as insolent

A) Loyal
B) Insistent
C) Silent
D) Rude

1 lakh

Q5 The Green Revolution was related to planting of trees.

True or False?

2 lakh

Q6 To make paper what is wood turned into?

5 lakh

Q7 The famous paintings in Bihar are called ___________.

A) Madhubani
B) Madhu divani
C) Shilpa kantha

10 lakh

Q8 The orbit around the sun is not quite round, it is ___________.

20 lakh

Q9 Spell the word... Colloquial.

50 lakh

Q10 How many plural nouns are in the following sentence ?

"Over the barn, geese flew between the raindrops."

1 Crore

Q11 4 Tripitakas are the sacred books of the...

A) Jains
B) Hindus
C) Muslims
D) Buddhists

5 Crore

Quiz 23

Q1 Is 0 a positive or negative number? 10,000/-

Q2 Which colour belt do the beginners in judo wear? 20,000/-

Q3 What do penguins use to make their nests? 50,000/-

Q4 Find a similar meaning word as crippled. 1 lakh

A) Blind
B) Deaf
C) Lame
D) Mad

Q5 The center of the Earth is known as ___________. 2 lakh

A) The lower mantle
B) The epicenter
C) The eye
D) The core

Q6 To make a cup of tea ratio of water to milk is 3:1. So to make 4 cups of tea what should be the ratio of water to milk? **5 lakh**

A) 4:3:1
B) 12:1
C) 12:4
D) 4:12

Q7 The Bhakra dam is across the ________. **10 lakh**

A) Sutlej
B) Ravi
C) Beas
D) Chenals Rivers

Q8 The least number that has to be subtracted from 22344 to make it divisible by 9 is ____. **20 lakh**

Q9 Raireshwar is famous for its ________ temples. **50 lakh**

Q10 How many colours are there in the National Flag of India? **1 Crore**

Q11 As per our constitution children below what age cannot be employed? **5 Crore**

Quiz 24

Q1 Khan saves Rs. 250 every month. How much money will he be saving in 1 year?

Q2 Which country is associated with Kangaroos?

Q3 What creatures have wings but to swim and not fly?

Q4 Dr. Sharma charges Rs. 42.00 for an office visit, which is 3/4 of what Dr. Pai charges. How much does Dr. Pai charge?

A) Rs. 52.50
B) Rs. 31.50
C) Rs. 56
D) Rs. 54

Q5 The ___________ parts of the plants are used as manure

A) Fresh
B) Green
C) Decayed
D) Thin

Q6 The title "Vikramaditiya" was assumed by...

A) Ashoka
B) Chandragupta II
C) Kanishka
D) Samudragupta

Q7 The ancient Roman empire was in which continent? 10 lakh

Q8 The fire cracker industry is located in... 20 lakh

A) Sivasaki
B) Kolar
C) Chennai

Q9 Pinocchio, from the Italian fairy tale by Carlo Collodi, does not appreciate the advice of the talking cricket. What does he do to the cricket to get him to stop giving him unwanted advice? 50 lakh

A) Traps him in a jar
B) Buries him in the garden
C) Throws a hammer at him
D) Feeds him to a crow

Q10 Name the machine on which fibre is woven to get cloth. 1 Crore

Q11 Blood is purified in the lungs.
True or False?

5 Crore

Quiz 25

Q1 3 x 133 = ? — 10,000/-

Q2 Which discovery lead to humans being able to travel to distant places faster and easier? — 20,000/-

Q3 What colour must be mixed with the colour of the clear sky to get the colour of the grass? — 50,000/-

Q4 Does a seed need warmth to grow? — 1 lakh

Yes / No

Q5 Suddenly the car changed directions...What is 'suddenly' - adjective or adverb? — 2 lakh

Q6 The Shivneri Fort is in which district of Maharashtra?

Q7 Swami and Friends was the first novel of which renowned writer?

A) R K Narayan
B) Khushwant Singh
C) Mulk Raj Anand
D) Swami Vivekanand

Q8 The earthquake is strongest at the _________.

Q9 On a mountain range, the side where the rain falls is called the __________.

Q10 Name the different sensory organs in human beings?

Q11 1 kilogram equals 2.2 pounds. If Brett weighs 189 pounds, what is his weight in kilograms?

A) 5.8 kgs
B) 207.9 kgs
C) 95.6 kgs
D) 85.9 kgs

Quiz 26

Q1 A figure with four sides is called an angle.

True or False?

Q2 Which English word is used most frequently in writing?

A) And
B) To
C) The
D) A

Q3 What are the primary colors in paints?

Q4 Cotton seed has hair that help it get carried by wind.

Yes / No

Q5 State the conjunction in the following sentence.

Maya likes orchids and violets.

Q6 The place where the river ends its journey is called ______.

Q7 Sum of 2 sides of a triangle is always ___________ than the third side.

Q8 The difference between 2 numbers is 4937. If the greater number is 30451, what is the small number?

20 lakh

Q9 Lakshwadeep has __________ islands.

A) 36
B) 10
C) 100

50 lakh

Q10 Large mass of moving ice is called Glacier...True or False?

True or False?

1 Crore

Q11 A captain wants to arrange his soldiers in such a way that the number of soldiers in each row is same as the number of rows. If there are 601 number of soldiers, how many soldiers will have to hold out?

A) 49
B) 36
C) 11
D) 25

5 Crore

Quiz 27

Q1 An article is sold at double its cost price. What is the gain percent? 10,000/-

Q2 Which indian exercise keeps us fit? (4 letters) 20,000/-

Q3 What animal is there in the symbol of WWF? 50,000/-

Q4 Cotton comes from a plant. Silk comes from ________. 1 lakh

Q5 Spell the word that means "full of beauty." 2 lakh

Q6 The name of which sport has been taken from the French word meaning shepherd's stick? 5 lakh

A) Tennis
B) Base Ball
C) Hockey
D) Cricket

Q7 Spell the word... Sovereign.

10 lakh

Q8 The Deccan Plateau is not surrounded by ________.

A) Western Ghats
B) Eastern Ghats
C) Vindhyas and Satpura
D) Rajmahal Hills

20 lakh

Q9 In which kind of sentence the clauses may be joined by a coordinating conjunction and a comma, by a semicolon alone, or by a conjunctive adverb and a semicolon?

A) Simple
B) Compound
C) Complex

50 lakh

Q10 India is in the Western Hempishere?

True or False?

1 Crore

Q11 1 million - 900 tens = ?

5 Crore

Quiz 28

Q1 Desert Storms are called ________.

A) Sandstorms
B) Hurricanes
C) Tornados
D) Avalanches

Q2 Which is India's national game?

Q3 What is the favourite food of the Panda bear?

Q4 Complete the sentence.

Half a crust is better than.

Q5 Spell the word pomegranate.

Q6 The Indo-Gangetic Plain is named after?

A) Yamuna & India.
B) Ganga & Indus rivers
C) Ganga & India

Q7 Sherlock Holmes. The name instantly brings to mind images of deductive powers, snappy clothing and a dull sidekick. Which of the following is a Holmes story?

A) A Study in Scarlet
B) The Mystery of Marie Roget
C) The Woman in White
D) Lord Jim

Q8 The dance form of Andhra Pradesh is ________.

A) Kuchipudi
B) Kathakali
C) Mohini-Attam
D) Bharatnatyam

Q9 In the Roman numeration system, there are only ______ basic numerals.

Q10 A ___________ of puppies.

Add the collective noun.

Q11 Which state in India means the Land of the Rising Sun ?

A) Mizoram
B) Arunachal Pradesh
C) Assam
D) Tripura

Quiz 29

Q1 Which is the highest land mountain in the world? 10,000/-

Q2 Which is the edible part of the potato? 20,000/-

Q3 Whales breathe through gills. 50,000/-
True / False

Q4 Complete the sentence. 1 lakh
A penny saved is _________.

Q5 Rahul's paternal aunt is Aarti's mother. How is Aarti related to Rahul? 2 lakh

Q6 The Indian subcontinent is __________.

A) Landlocked
B) Peninsula
C) Island
D) Archipelago

5 lakh

10 lakh

Q7 Of which monument are the Delhi Gate and the Lahori Gate the two main entrances?

20 lakh

Q8 The broad steps cut into hills are called __________.

50 lakh

Q9 In the following series find the one which does not belong to the group? II, III, V, VII, IX, XI, XIII, XVII.

1 Crore

Q10 8:20 pm in 24 hr clock is__________.

Q11 As cheerful as...

Complete this Figure of Speech

5 Crore

Quiz 30

Q1 Spell the missing word: — 10,000/-

"There are no essays on the test. It's all multiple________."

Q2 Which is the largest type of bear? — 20,000/-

Q3 We keep fish in this 8 letter home. Spell it. — 50,000/-

Q4 Complete the following...Rats desert a sinking... — 1 lakh

Q5 In words like telephone, telegram, television, etc what does the term 'tele' mean? — 2 lakh

Q6 The Golden Temple was built by which Sikh Guru? — 5 lakh

A) Guru Nanak
B) Guru Arjun Dev
C) Guru Gobind Singh
D) Guru Ram Das

Q7 In which year were the first atom bombs dropped on Hiroshima and Nagasaki ?

10 lakh

A) 1941
B) 1946
C) 1945
D) 1944

Q8 Sum of two integers is +62. If one of the integer is -48, then what is the other integer?

20 lakh

Q9 In how many years will Rs. 2000 double at the rate of 5% p.a.?

50 lakh

Q10 12 o'clock in the night is written as 12:00 PM.

1 Crore

True or False?

Q11 What is the Volcano in Andaman's called?

A) Barren
B) Latur
C) Port Blair
D) Spring

5 Crore

Quiz 31

Q1 What is the opposite of 'expensive'?

Q2 Which is the most widely found mammal on earth?

A) Bat
B) Whale
C) Monkey
D) Human

Q3 These numbers make a pattern guess the next number? 130, 110, 90, 70, _____.

Q4 China is in the western hemisphere.

True or False?

Q5 In which year did the first man land on the moon?

2 lakh

Q6 The difference between 7 hrs 25 minutes and 3 hrs 45 minutes is ________________.

5 lakh

Q7 In which year was the Indian National Congress founded?

10 lakh

Q8 Srinagar is situated on______.

A) Jhelum
B) Chenab
C) Ravi
D) Beas

20 lakh

Q9 If you wind up an eight -day clock on the 1st of January, how many times will you have had to wind up by the 2nd March in a leap year?

50 lakh

Q10 (4x8) + (9x5) = ?

1 Crore

Q11 A potato is also a __________.

A) Seed
B) Nut
C) Tuber
D) Stem

5 Crore

Quiz 32

Q1 What is the opposite of gloomy? 10,000/-

Q2 Which is the only mammal that can fly? 20,000/-

Q3 There are three people in a room. If they cut an apple into 3 equal pieces and take 1 piece each, each has eaten what part of the apple? 50,000/-

A) 1
B) Half
C) One-third
D) One-fourth

Q4 Chandigarh is the common capital of Punjab and _______? 1 lakh

Q5 If you spell write as right, what is it? 2 lakh

Q6 The correct term for a naming word is? 5 lakh

Q7 In which system of the human body are the lungs?

A) Respiratory
B) Digestive
C) Circulatory
D) Nervous

Q8 Spiders are eight-legged insects.

True or False?

Q9 If there are 8 mangoes in 1 bag, how many are there in 15 such bags? If we take out 30 of them how many will be left?

A) 80
B) 90
C) 100
D) 70

Q10 (3x4) is the same as (3x3x3x3).

True or False?

Q11 A bottlenose dolphin is a fish.

True or False?

Quiz 33

Q1 What is the meaning of 'underneath'? — 10,000/-

Q2 Which is the Pink City in India? — 20,000/-

Q3 The Pacific Ocean is the second largest Ocean in the world. — 50,000/-

True or False?

Q4 By which other name is soccer known? — 1 lakh

Q5 If the length and breadth of a rectangular ground is 60 meters and 30 meters respectively, what is it's perimeter? — 2 lakh

Q6 The Amazon is the longest river in the world.

True or False?

Q7 In which language did Babur write his autobiography titled Babur Nama?

A) Urdu
B) Sanskrit
C) Hindi
D) Turkish

Q8 Shivaji got married at the age of_____.

A) 4
B) 14
C) 24
D) 44

Q9 If a square piece of paper has an area of 25 sqcms, what are the lengths of the sides?

Q10 A silver jubilee stands for the 25th anniversary. What stands for the 60th anniversary?

Q11 Name 2 birds that cannot fly. Each name has 7 letters.

Quiz 34

Q1 Asia is a country located to the south of Europe. 10,000/-

True or False?

Q2 Which is the world's most populated country? 20,000/-

Q3 The outermost layer of the Earth is called the _____. 50,000/-

A) Upper mantle
B) Lower Mantle
C) Soil
D) Crust

Q4 Between 1 and 100, how many multiples of 5 are odd numbers ? 1 lakh

Q5 If a fireman is pumping water from a 10,000 litre tank at the rate of 250 litres a minute, how long will the supply last? 2 lakh

Q6 S Ramanujam was a renowned Indian economist?

True or False?

5 lakh

Q7 In which city is the White House (residence of the U.S. President) located?

10 lakh

Q8 Saturn is made of primarily two gases - hydrogen and...

A) Helium
B) Lithium
C) Nitrogen
D) Methane

20 lakh

Q9 How much time is taken by the minute hand to cover an angle 54° from its initial position?

50 lakh

Q10 A noun is the name of a person, place, thing or idea.

True or False?

1 Crore

Q11 Are pine, cedar and spruce evergreen trees.

Yes / No

5 Crore

Quiz 35

Q1 Himalayas are the oldest mountain range in the world. 10,000/-

True or False?

Q2 Which letter of the English alphabet occurs least often while writing? 20,000/-

Q3 The Great Indian Desert is also called _______. 50,000/-

A) Thar
B) Sahara

Q4 As old as... 1 lakh

Complete this Figure of Speech.

Q5 Hyderabad city exists in Pakistan as well.

True or False?

Q6 On which date is World Environment Day observed?

Q7 In Hindu mythology, who made the river Ganga decend on earth?

Q8 Which season do Rabi crops grow in?

Q9 How many spokes are there in the wheel of the Indian national flag?

Q10 A bird in hand is worth _____ in the bush.

Fill in the blank.

Q11 About whom did Sir Donald Bradman say, "He reminds me of myself"?

Quiz 36

Q1 What color would you mix with red to get the color pink? 10,000/-

Q2 Which month does not have the same number of days every year? 20,000/-

Q3 The common factors of 12 and 15 are. 50,000/-

Q4 As greedy as a...

Complete this Figure of Speech. 1 lakh

Q5 How will you express 19 in Roman numbers? 2 lakh

Q6 Kamla Nehru was one of the women participants in the Civil Disobedience Movement.

True or False? 5 lakh

Q7 If Dialogue is spelt this way in British English, how is it spelt in American English?

10 lakh

Q8 Pick out the adjectives in the following sentence.

Nishi is a wonderful painter as well as a talented singer.

20 lakh

Q9 How many lanes are there in an Olympic swimming pool ?

A) 5
B) 6
C) 7
D) 8

50 lakh

Q10 Do twins have identical fingerprints?

Yes / No

1 Crore

Q11 ______ is thicker than water.

Complete the famous saying...

Quiz 37

Q1 What color would you mix with red to get the colour maroon? 10,000/-

Q2 Which of the following does an insect definitely have? 20,000/-

A) Six legs
B) Wings
C) Spots on their body
D) None of the above

Q3 The air near the sea coast is generally dry. 50,000/-

True or False?

Q4 As cunning as a... 1 lakh

Complete this Figure of Speech.

Q5 How do the muscles move the arm up and down? 2 lakh

Q6 In which cave complex in western India are 12 Buddhist caves, 17 Hindu caves and 5 Jain caves? 5 lakh

Q7 How old was Alexander the Great when he died in 323 B.C.? 10 lakh

Q8 Invertebrate animals have no ________.

20 lakh

A) Legs
B) Tail
C) Spine
D) Bladder

Q9 How many countries are there in the world?

50 lakh

Q10 By what river is Lucknow situated?

1 Crore

A) Gomti
B) Gangotri
C) Yamuna
D) Beas

Q11 A cubical dice has six faces and has 1 to 6 dots on its faces. To obtain a total of 19, what is the minimum number of times the dice is to be thrown?

A) 4
B) 3
C) 5
D) 6

5 Crore

Quiz 38

Q1 Who was the first Prime Minister of independent India? 10,000/-

Q2 Which of the following is not a pest? 20,000/-

A) Flea
B) Termite
C) Locust
D) Butterfly

Q3 Take 7.34 from 9.09. 50,000/-

Q4 As ________ as a toad. 1 lakh

Complete this Figure of Speech

Q5 During monsoon dark clouds are seen in the sky...What part of speech is the word dark? 2 lakh

A) Adjective
B) Noun
C) Pronoun
D) Verb

Q6 How many proper nouns are in the following sentence ? 5 lakh

"In Asansol, Anita met my aunt, Anuradha."

Q7 How many stanzas are there in the National Anthem of India?

Q8 If your small sister's bricks are 10 cms high, how many will she need to build a tower 1 and 1/2 metres high?

Q9 How many articles are in the following sentence?

"I went to the fruit stand and bought a banana and an apple."

Q10 About what percentage of India's working population is engaged in agriculture?

A) 80%
B) 75%
C) 70%
D) 60%

Q11 How long is the Great Wall of China?

A) 3,000 km
B) 2,400 km
C) 2,000 km
D) 2,500 km

Quiz 39

Q1 If it is 2:43 P.M., how many minutes will it be until the school bell rings at 3.00 P.M?

Q2 Which of these is the world's heaviest land animal?

A) Hippopotamus
B) Rhinoceros
C) African elephant
D) Polar bear

Q3 State the types of nouns in the following sentence.

Today Alek saw many dogs at the park.

Q4 Are these numbers 3:27, 9:9 in proportion?

Q5 Complete the sentence.

A small leak will...

Q6 How many horses take part in a water polo?

A) Two
B) Six
C) Eleven
D) None

Q7 How many millimeters in 17.5 centimetres?

Q8 How much of the human body is composed of water?

A) One-third
B) Two-third
C) Three-fourth
D) One-fifth

Q9 How many adjectives are there in this sentence ?

"My brown dog grabbed the bleached bone in his wet mouth."

Q10 Besides India, which other country celebrates its Independence Day on August 15?

Q11 If 8 children that is $1/4^{th}$ of the class is absent. What is the total of the class?

Quiz 40

Q1 If one can contains 18 kgs of oil, how much oil is there in 30 cans?

A) 48 kgs
B) 540 kgs
C) 54 kgs
D) 5400 kgs

Q2 Which one is a wrongly spelt word...refill, bangel, circle, middle.

Q3 State the adjectives in the following sentence.

The small boat floats on the dark sea

Q4 An octagon is a shape with how many sides?

Q5 Complete the following...Barking dogs...

Q6 How many days does the moon take to revolve round the earth ?

A) 281/5
B) 301/4
C) 291/2
D) 271/3

Q7 How many articles are found in the following sentence ?

"The rabbit jumped into the hole."

10 lakh

Q8 How many spokes does the chakra on the Indian flag have?

20 lakh

Q9 How do snakes protect themselves from danger?

50 lakh

Q10 As __________ as Vinegar.

Complete this Figure of Speech

1 Crore

Q11 If two angles are supplementary to each other, then which of the following is completely true?

A) Both angles are obtuse
B) Both angles are acute
C) The sum of both angles is less than 180°
D) One angle is acute and other is obtuse

5 Crore

Quiz 41

Q1 If there are in 11 questions per quiz in this book and there are 75 quizzes, how many questions are in this book? 10,000/-

Q2 Which organs of the flowering plants take in water? 20,000/-

Q3 Spell the missing word: The Rockies are a range of _____. 50,000/-

Q4 Add 62 and 59 and divide by 11. 1 lakh

Q5 Complete the following sentence. 2 lakh

Dry as a _____.

Q6 How many consonants are there in the following word.

Cricket

Q7 Herbivores have sharp claws.

True or False?

Q8 How many Gurus have been there in Sikhism?

Q9 For which game is Prakash Padukone famous?

Q10 After which pillar is the National Emblem of India designed?

Q11 What was Thailand's previous name?

Quiz 42

Q1 123 x 23 x 0 = ? — 10,000/-

Q2 Which places are likely to have houses with sloping roofs? — 20,000/-

Q3 Soil in river beds is ____. — 50,000/-

A) Red
B) Sandy
C) Clayey
D) Loam

Q4 Add 45 and 39 and divide by 7. — 1 lakh

Q5 By which other name is the storage unit of a computer known? — 2 lakh

Q6 How are birds and humans similar? — 5 lakh

Q7 Frankenstein. The very word immediately makes one think of the word 'monster'. Who is the Author of this classic? — 10 lakh

A) Mary Shelley
B) Wilkie Collins
C) Bram Stoker
D) Louisa May Alcott

Q8 How many adverbs are in the sentence ? — 20 lakh

"Our portly dad belches loudly."

Q9 Estimate the product of 20 x 30 x 80. — 50 lakh

Q10 20 years ago, when my parents got married, their age was 23 years, now the average age of my family, consisting of myself and my parents only is 35 years. What is my present age? — 1 Crore

Q11 Name the class of animals that eat grass? — 5 Crore

Quiz 43

Q1 240 minutes is equal to how many hours? 10,000/-

Q2 Which two colors do you blend together to make orange. 20,000/-

Q3 Rabri Devi was the Chief Minister of which state? 50,000/-

Q4 A, E, I, O and U are known as what? 1 lakh

Q5 At what time did India get freedom? 2 lakh

A) 6.00 p.m.
B) At noon
C) At midnight
D) 10.00 a.m.

Q6 Find a similar meaning word as miscreant. 5 lakh

A) Naughty
B) Disobedient
C) Villian
D) Well-behaved

Q7 Dante was the Italian philosopher who wrote Divine Comedy.

True or False?

10 lakh

Q8 How many adjectives are in the following sentence?

"The principal is a beautiful woman."

20 lakh

Q9 Circumference of a circle is approximately equal to _______ diameter.

A) 4 time
B) 6 times
C) 3 times
D) 5 times

50 lakh

Q10 Difference of sums of 998 and -486 from 290 and 732.

1 Crore

Q11 April showers brings ________ flowers.

Fill in the blank.

5 Crore

Answers

Quiz 1

Q1 Bombay, Calcutta & Madras
Q2 Oxygen
Q3 D) Ears
Q4 C) Rs. 14.25
Q5 C) Heart
Q6 Orbit
Q7 Briskly
Q8 Calcium and Phosphate
Q9 NASA
Q10 Skin
Q11 C) Smallpox

Quiz 2

Q1 Louder
Q2 Hindi
Q3 0.274
Q4 B) 24
Q5 Movement
Q6 The Golden Temple
Q7 Rocks and humus
Q8 They help plants reproduce
Q9 Tableland
Q10 A) Punjab & Sind
Q11 True

Quiz 3

Q1 Saucers
Q2 Oxen
Q3 Sun
Q4 B) Clumsy
Q5 D) Cyclone
Q6 Occassionally
Q7 Volume
Q8 1800
Q9 Muster
Q10 A) 1853
Q11 False - It is used to measure the depth of oceans

Quiz 4

Q1 C) Bird
Q2 10
Q3 Jakarta
Q4 4976
Q5 B) Sphinx
Q6 Linguist
Q7 B) Gomukh
Q8 Vixen
Q9 D) 2.5 acres
Q10 Square
Q11 D) Sikkim

Quiz 5

Q1 A) 350
Q2 Marble
Q3 Product
Q4 C) 45
Q5 Verb
Q6 Egoist
Q7 C) President & Two Houses
Q8 Starch
Q9 In good faith
Q10 A) Deciduous
Q11 900m

Quiz 6

Q1 1 line
Q2 Fawn
Q3 Blue
Q4 High Court
Q5 World Wildlife Fund
Q6 Don't worry about difficulties unless they actually occur
Q7 Exempli gratia (for example)
Q8 Sofia
Q9 Scientific
Q10 B) Two
Q11 B) A Tale of Two Cities

Quiz 7

Q1 1.5
Q2 Eaglet
Q3 117

Q4 10
Q5 Beak
Q6 Line of symmetry
Q7 District of Columbia
Q8 Food stored in different parts of the plant
Q9 A huddle
Q10 2
Q11 C) 5,000

Quiz 8

Q1 0.33
Q2 Owlet
Q3 Dew
Q4 Chips
Q5 Cows swallow their food and fill their stomach. Later they bring it back to their mouths and keep chewing for hours.
Q6 Cape Comorin
Q7 Carbon dioxide and manure
Q8 Radii
Q9 Nippon
Q10 6
Q11 Interior opposite

Quiz 9

Q1 12
Q2 A) Flowers
Q3 Myanmar
Q4 Increases
Q5 Standard Time
Q6 Hardware
Q7 A) Vaigai & Kaveri
Q8 D) Short delivery
Q9 Talons
Q10 18
Q11 A) Greek

Quiz 10

Q1 47
Q2 Elections
Q3 2
Q4 6
Q5 Insectivorous Plants
Q6 B) To honour promising young people
Q7 D) Narmada
Q8 Angle $> 180^\circ$ and $< 360^\circ$
Q9 Remains of living things found deep under layers of rock
Q10 3
Q11 Still

Quiz 11

Q1 Compass
Q2 Ballerinas
Q3 Baking Powder
Q4 2
Q5 Purple
Q6 Itanagar
Q7 False
Q8 Vertex
Q9 1hr
Q10 C) Nepal
Q11 Exercise Book

Quiz 12

Q1 1
Q2 Netaji
Q3 A) Line
Q4 20
Q5 Consolation Prize
Q6 Snow slides off easily
Q7 False - Nuclear Power
Q8 Bombay Natural History Society
Q9 Fungi
Q10 Clock
Q11 A) 175

Quiz 13

Q1 Square
Q2 Hey Ram
Q3 Plateau
Q4 3600
Q5 Lyrics

Answers

Q6 A plant that depends on another plant for food
Q7 B) Reptiles
Q8 A rafter
Q9 C) 36,54, 72
Q10 Sachin Tendulkar
Q11 90 km/ hr

Quiz 14

Q1 Right angle triangle
Q2 City
Q3 Programmer
Q4 3
Q5 Red, blue, yellow
Q6 Dermatologist
Q7 Buddhism
Q8 A spiderling
Q9 Carefully
Q10 500 litres
Q11 False - Groundnuts

Quiz 15

Q1 1
Q2 School
Q3 B) Florist
Q4 They tell us where animals live
Q5 North Pole, 90 degrees North; South Pole, 90 degrees South
Q6 School
Q7 A) 7
Q8 True
Q9 An obtuse angle
Q10 D) Janus
Q11 C) Mamallapuram

Quiz 16

Q1 No
Q2 B) Stems
Q3 Radius
Q4 They huddle together
Q5 Degrees
Q6 Bamboo
Q7 C) Saraswati
Q8 False
Q9 C) Narmada
Q10 84 cm
Q11 D) Argon & Nitrogen

Quiz 17

Q1 Rs. 2200
Q2 Pears,apples,bananas
Q3 Knock at the Door
Q4 C) By eating plants
Q5 Morals
Q6 C) Chlorophyll
Q7 Puri, Orissa
Q8 Bodhi
Q9 B) Hymns
Q10 Constellation
Q11 Consignment

Quiz 18

Q1 One
Q2 Library
Q3 C) Animals
Q4 A) Through their skin
Q5 Silica (Sand)
Q6 Food and oxygen
Q7 Chilka
Q8 False - They are caused by the gravitional pull of the moon
Q9 A) St. Francis Xavier
Q10 20
Q11 A) 40

Quiz 19

Q1 21
Q2 Cinema or theatre
Q3 B) A twig
Q4 Careless
Q5 Termites
Q6 A) Shivalik
Q7 A) 1510
Q8 C) Oxygen
Q9 Antarctica
Q10 B) Cockroach
Q11 A) Odissi

Quiz 20

Q1 D) 70
Q2 July and August
Q3 Green
Q4 Railway tracks
Q5 C) Brahmaputra
Q6 Carnivores
Q7 1001
Q8 C) Hampi
Q9 B) Dhyan Chand
Q10 Stem
Q11 A) A method of dyeing

Quiz 21

Q1 21
Q2 Owl
Q3 A charm
Q4 Spider
Q5 False - Earth
Q6 Kite Flying
Q7 False - Bombay and Thane
Q8 Oxygen, minerals
Q9 V
Q10 Letter e
Q11 D) Ranchi

Quiz 22

Q1 9
Q2 Mumbai
Q3 Stethoscope
Q4 D) Rude
Q5 False
Q6 Pulp
Q7 A) Madhubani
Q8 Eliptical
Q9 C-O-L-L-O-Q-U-I-A-L
Q10 2
Q11 D) Buddhists

Quiz 23

Q1 Neither negative nor positive
Q2 White
Q3 Pebbles
Q4 C) Lame
Q5 D) The core
Q6 C) 12:4
Q7 A) Sutlej
Q8 6
Q9 Shiva
Q10 4
Q11 14

Quiz 24

Q1 3000
Q2 Australia
Q3 Penguins
Q4 C) Rs. 56
Q5 C) Decayed
Q6 B) Chandragupta II
Q7 Europe
Q8 A) Sivasaki
Q9 C) Throws a hammer at him
Q10 Loom
Q11 False - Heart

Quiz 25

Q1 399
Q2 Wheel
Q3 Yellow
Q4 Yes
Q5 Adverb
Q6 Pune
Q7 A) R K Narayan
Q8 Epicenter
Q9 Windward side
Q10 Eyes, Ears, Nose, Tounge and Skin
Q11 D) 85.9 kgs

Quiz 26

Q1 False - Quadrilateral, Square, Rectangle
Q2 C) The
Q3 Red, blue, yellow
Q4 Yes
Q5 And-conjunction
Q6 Mouth
Q7 Greater than

Answers

Q8 25514
Q9 A) 36
Q10 True
Q11 D) 25

Quiz 27

Q1 50%
Q2 Yoga
Q3 Panda
Q4 Silkworm
Q5 Beautiful
Q6 C) Hockey
Q7 S-O-V-E-R-E-I-G-N
Q8 D) Rajmahal Hills
Q9 B) Compound
Q10 False
Q11 991000

Quiz 28

Q1 A) Sandstorms
Q2 Hockey
Q3 Bamboo
Q4 No bread
Q5 Pomegranate
Q6 B) Ganga & Indus rivers
Q7 A) A Study in Scarlet
Q8 A) Kuchipudi
Q9 7
Q10 Litter
Q11 B) Arunachal Pradesh

Quiz 29

Q1 Mount Everest
Q2 Tuber or underground stem
Q3 False
Q4 A penny gained
Q5 Paternal Cousins
Q6 B) Peninsula
Q7 Red Fort
Q8 Terraces
Q9 IX
Q10 20:20
Q11 A Lark

Quiz 30

Q1 Choice
Q2 Polar
Q3 Aquarium
Q4 Ship
Q5 Far
Q6 B) Guru Arjun Dev
Q7 C) 1945
Q8 110
Q9 20 years
Q10 False - 12:00 AM
Q11 A) Barren

Quiz 31

Q1 Cheap
Q2 D) Human
Q3 50
Q4 False
Q5 1969
Q6 3 hrs 40 min
Q7 1885
Q8 A) Jhelum
Q9 8
Q10 77
Q11 C) Tuber

Quiz 32

Q1 Happy
Q2 Bat
Q3 C) One-third
Q4 Harayana
Q5 Wrong
Q6 Noun
Q7 A) Respiratory
Q8 False - they are not insects
Q9 B) 90
Q10 False
Q11 False

Quiz 33

Q1 Below
Q2 Jaipur
Q3 False - It is the largest

Q4 Football
Q5 180 meters
Q6 False - Amazon is widest.
Q7 D) Turkish
Q8 14
Q9 5cm x5cm
Q10 Diamond Jubilee
Q11 Ostrich and Penguin

Quiz 34

Q1 False
Q2 China
Q3 D) Crust
Q4 10
Q5 40 mins
Q6 False - He was a Mathematician
Q7 Washington D.C.
Q8 A) Helium
Q9 9 min
Q10 True
Q11 Yes

Quiz 35

Q1 False
Q2 Z
Q3 A) Thar
Q4 Hills
Q5 True
Q6 June 5th
Q7 Bhagiratha
Q8 Winter
Q9 24
Q10 Two
Q11 Sachin Tendulkar

Quiz 36

Q1 White
Q2 February
Q3 1 and 3
Q4 Dog
Q5 XIX
Q6 True
Q7 Dialog
Q8 A) Wonderful
B) Talented
Q9 D) 8
Q10 No
Q11 Blood

Quiz 37

Q1 Black
Q2 A) Six legs
Q3 False - Humid
Q4 Fox
Q5 They expand and contract
Q6 Ellora Caves
Q7 33 Years
Q8 C) Spine
Q9 212 countries
Q10 A) Gomti
Q11 A) 4

Quiz 38

Q1 Jawaharlal Nehru
Q2 D) Butterfly
Q3 1.75
Q4 Ugly
Q5 A) Adjective
Q6 3
Q7 Five
Q8 15
Q9 3
Q10 C) 70%
Q11 B) 2,400 km

Quiz 39

Q1 17
Q2 C) African elephant
Q3 Alek-Proper noun, Dogs-Plural noun, Park-Common noun
Q4 No
Q5 Sink a great ship
Q6 D) None
Q7 175
Q8 C) Three-fourth
Q9 3
Q10 South Korea
Q11 32

Answers

Quiz 40

Q1 B) 540 kgs
Q2 Bangel
Q3 Small, dark-Adjectives
Q4 8
Q5 Seldom bite
Q6 D) 271/3
Q7 2
Q8 24
Q9 They pretend to be dead
Q10 Sour
Q11 D) One angle is acute and other is obtuse

Quiz 41

Q1 825
Q2 Roots
Q3 Mountains
Q4 11
Q5 Bone
Q6 Five
Q7 False
Q8 10
Q9 Badminton
Q10 Ashoka Pillar at Sarnath
Q11 Siam

Quiz 42

Q1 0
Q2 Rainy and snowy areas
Q3 B) Sandy
Q4 12
Q5 Hard disk
Q6 They are both warm blooded
Q7 A) Mary Shelley
Q8 2
Q9 48000
Q10 19 years
Q11 Herbivorous

Quiz 43

Q1 4 hours
Q2 Yellow and red
Q3 Bihar
Q4 vowels
Q5 C) At midnight
Q6 C) Villian
Q7 True
Q8 1
Q9 C) 3 times
Q10 510
Q11 May